PSYCHOLOGY IN A NUTSHELL

THIRTY THINGS THAT WILL HELP YOU UNDERSTAND THE SCIENCE OF PSYCHOLOGY

BY

BRADLEY W. RASCH

PREFACE

—⚮—

Everybody wants to understand psychology. Most of us fancy ourselves to be experts on human behavior; we are, after all, human, we behave, so we are qualified.

The discipline of psychology is vast, and ever expanding, especially in light of recent breakthroughs such as the human genome project, research on the brain, and an impressive volume of studies conducted primarily here, in the United States. The field of psychology is expanding its knowledge base at a faster pace than any other science, with the possible exceptions of genetics and computer science.

Still, it is possible to get a grasp of the field by looking closely at its thirty most important concepts.

This book will attempt to give you a feel for the science of psychology by looking it's thirty most important concepts, theories, people, or ideas in this vital and interesting field.

Let's get started.

TABLE OF CONTENTS

—ɯ—

1

WILHELM WUNDT
(1832-1920)

—〰—

By the 1870's, a small group of scholars from the fields of philosophy and physiology began posing questions about the mind, sensation, and human behavior. Psychology, as an independent academic discipline, did not exist, as we know it today.

Along came Wilhelm Wundt of Germany. He campaigned for psychology to become an independent area of study from his position as a professor in Leipzig, Germany. Science was in vogue, the time was right, and he was successful in his campaign to have psychology become an independent area of academic study.

But Wundt was not finished. He insisted that psychology become a "hard science", like physics or chemistry, and that it adhere to the principles of the scientific method, and that it be empirical.

Wundt established the first psychological research laboratory, and the first scientific journal devoted to psychology.

Wundt saw the primary focus of psychology to be the study of consciousness. Psychology, as a field of study, began to research our conscious experiences and the relationship between the mind and the body, and did so in a way that was compatible with the scientific processes of the times.

Wundt was a prolific researcher and writer, and many of the first generation psychologists trained under him and fanned out across the world, especially to the United States, and started their own psychological research projects and academic departments. One of them, G. Stanley Hall, became the father of *American* psychology, much like Wundt himself who is credited with being the father of the science. (Bet you thought it was Freud before reading this).

The favorite research technique of Wundt and psychology's founding fathers was introspection. This method of research required the people that were involved in experiments to: report the content of their conscious experiences, to talk about how and why they made the decisions they did, and how they experienced the things they experienced, during the experiments. This technique required these "introspectionists" to be highly trained, and was considered to be cutting edge research methodology at the time. In modern times, this approach is not considered to be scientific at all. But it was, in the day, a way to start.

2

SIGMUND FREUD
AND PSYCHOANALYSIS

—⁓—

Sigmund Freud, an Austrian physician born in Freiberg, Moravia, lived from 1856-1939. This made all of his talk about sex and the unconscious remarkable. Such things simply were not discussed in polite society in his day.

It is a little known fact that Freud was a heavy user of cocaine. Perhaps this explains some of the terms he coined, such as "penis envy". In Freud's defense, in his day, the substance was commonly used, and even prescribed by physicians.

Though an oversimplification, it can be said that Freud's theory of psycho-analysis suggests that unconscious forces play an extraordinarily important role in forming our behavior, and are also the cause of a great deal of mental illness.

Freud believed that three forces within us determine our personality: 1. The Id-, which is driven by the libido, our sex drive, operates on the pleasure principle. This is the part of us that is selfish, that wants, no matter who may be hurt. 2. The superego-which is our conscience, our moral compass, if you will. 3. The ego- is the part of us the world sees. It operates on the reality principle. The ego deals with pressure from the id and superego to help us navigate through life. Sometimes the ego is made to feel guilty by the superego. **It is fair to say that it is the job of the ego to have the needs of the id met in a way that is acceptable to the superego**

Freud also brought to light the concept of defense mechanisms, as another example of unconscious forces. Defense mechanisms deny or distort reality so as to make it less threatening. We are not aware that we are using them.

One of many examples of a defense mechanism is sour grapes rationalization. An extremely shy boy for years tried to ask out a girl on a date. He finally mustered up the wherewithal to do so. She declined his invitation. Rather than being crushed, he tells himself that he didn't really want to go out with her anyway. Another example of a defense mechanism is projection. We see our faults in others so that we do not have to see them in ourselves. Defense mechanisms deny or distort reality so as to make it less threatening. And we are not aware that we are using them.

Perhaps the most important of defense mechanisms describes best what psychoanalysis is all about vis-à-vis unconscious forces. That defense mechanism is repression. When something very bad, very traumatic, happens to us, we bury it (repress it) so deep within our unconsciousness it as though it did not happen. Until we remember that event, and experience the emotions we repressed, we will have all kinds of emotional (and even physical) issues. Getting that memory out, unrepressing it, is the purpose of psychoanalysis. When we get that repressed memory out into our consciousness, and deal with it, we can presumably, come to grips with it and be made whole.

Freud's theory of psychoanalysis, and the power of the unconscious, has made a significant impact on the field of psychology. However, today we know that his theories are not scientifically testable, that the patients he based it on were not representative of the entire population, and that he may have distorted his research to support his theories.

3

VYGOTSKY AND HIS "ZONE"

—⟋⟍—

Lev Vygotsky(1896-1934) died young, at age 37, having made tremendous contributions to psychology by helping us understand how children learn.

Vygotsky viewed children as "little apprentices", who learn through "guided collaboration" with people who already have learned certain skills. Vygotsky's work is especially important in understanding cognitive psychology, and is widely studied by educational psychologists, and educators in general.

Vygotsky viewed learning as a social endeavor, and saw a child's social interactions with their parents (their most important teachers) and teachers as being of paramount importance to a child's quest for autonomy.

Children learn skills by imitation, observation, and through guided practice with others that are more knowledgeable and experienced.

Vygotsky's "zone of proximal development" refers to the gap between what a child already knows or can do independently and what they can do with the guidance of a parent, teacher, or other adult.

Vygotsky believed intelligence tests to be poor measures of a child's abilities because they assess only what a child knows, not what a child could know with assistance and nurturing.

Parents and teachers can provide a "scaffold", or context, so children can use knowledge they do have and apply it to new situations in problem solving.

4

JEAN PIAGET AND COGNITIVE DECELOPMENT

—✺—

Jean Piaget's theory is the grandfather of all cognitive development theories, because it was the first. Many of the terms and concepts he coined are still utilized extensively in cognitive psychology and developmental psychology to this day.

Piaget, 1896-1980, felt that children develop their thinking skills in stages.

The first stage, the sensori-motor stage takes place ages 0-2. Children learn using their senses, by navigating their environment (using their motor skills). In this first stage a child sees things and acts upon them. At the tail end of this stage, a child learns that an unseen object still exists.

The second stage, the pre-operational stage, occurs between ages 2-7. During this stage children develop language, and embrace it's symbolic nature. They also develop a facility with mental images. In this stage of cognitive development, a child is normally very "egocentric". In cognitive theory this means that a child can only see things from his or her perspective, and assumes everyone views the world as they do.

The third stage, the concrete operational stage lasts from ages 7-11. A child's thinking process becomes much less egocentric during this period of cognitive development.

Finally, a person achieves the last stage of cognitive development during the formal operational period, ages 11-15. During this stage, a child can think abstractly, ponder hypothetical issues, and entertain "contrary to the fact hypothesis". In other words, if you ask a child at this stage of development "what would the world be like if snow was green?" they could give you a rather sophisticated and thorough answer. Prior to this stage of development they could not, because snow is not green.

Piaget's work is not really scientific by *today's* standards, but it did start the conversation, and all cognitive development theories are still compared to his, which was the first theory of cognitive development.

5

ORDINAL POSITION OF BIRTH

—ⵡ—

Birth order, and its impact on ones personality and psychological development, is one of the most researched areas of psychology.

Many early psychologists believed that ones personality is significantly influenced by birth order. However, research does not really support this popular belief. Early studies of this issue did not really take into account *confounding variables* (factors or conditions other than birth order) that could influence a person's personality.

Alfred Adler, a prominent psychologist in the 1930's, suggested that the first-born child is often dominant, but that they tend to seek approval because they are soon "unthroned" by the birth of siblings. He believed the middle child is often competitive and learns how to negotiate well, and that the youngest child can be self-centered and demanding because they are used to being catered to.

Certainly a first-born child receives a great deal of attention because they have no competitors. When a sibling is born, the competition for attention begins, and the first-born acquires a new status.

Adler eventually amended his thoughts and indicated that ones environment, especially factors such as socioeconomic status, is a strong contributor to personality development. There is no doubt that birth order does influence ones personality development, just not as much as was earlier postulated.

More recent well-designed studies show that lower ranking in the birth order may have a very slight, and negative, effect on a persons intelligence quotient.

If birth order is as important as first suggested, what implications might that have for China, which currently has a one-child policy?

6

POSITIVE PSYCHOLOGY

—⟋⟍—

Psychology is often criticized for concentrating on the negative: mental illness, negative personality traits, and the like. The great philosopher Nietzsche famously said "What doesn't kill us makes us stronger." Positive psychology is a movement that focuses on the positive aspects of human behavior, and is directed towards moving psychology along those lines. Positive psychology involves self-help research, and looking at the positive aspects of human behavior.

Certainly, human beings do good things for one another, and these activities should be researched and explored. We are made stronger by dealing with adversity, and this is a proper area to research.

Certainly, relationships blossom, employees are more productive, and people are happier when they interact with positive, optimistic people.

Martin Seligman is credited with creating the positive psychology movement with his 1998 address to the American Psychological Association.

7

PLASTICITY OF THE BRAIN

—ᗯ—

Just by reading this sentence, you are changing your brain. You are encoding in your neurons (brain cells) information contained in this book, and that information will connect with other things you have learned. The brain is remarkably plastic. That means it can, and does, change. If part of the brain is damaged due to disease or injury, other parts of the brain can compensate for that damage, and take over the necessary functions.

The more we learn, the more active we are cognitively, the more our brain physically changes. With physical skills we "use it or loose it." This principle applies to our cognitive skills as well.

As we get older, it is important to remain not only physically active, but intellectually active as well. This, along with general physical health, is the best way too mitigate any cognitive loss that sometimes may otherwise occur with aging.

London cab drivers, who must pass an extremely demanding test to be licensed (which requires them to be able to find *any* location in the city), have brains that are physically changed due to their intense study regimen. This physical change of the brain produces many neuro-connections that allow them to learn many related tasks much more efficiently.

With the advent of GPS devices, will the London cabbies be "dumbed down"? In some ways, yes.

8

HARRY HARLOWE AND
HIS MONKEY BUSINESS

—ɱ—

Harry Harlowe had an interest in researching the bonds between mother and child. As is often the case in psychology, he started his research with animals.

Harlowe's chimps were "raised" by a wire mesh surrogate mother rigged up to dispense milk, or a soft cloth surrogate monkey that did not give out milk but provided soft comforting touch.

The baby monkeys preferred the soft cloth mother to the wire mesh mother, even though the cloth surrogate mother did not provide nourishment. Further, the baby chimps that spent more time with the cloth mother were more secure, interacted better with other monkeys, and were less frightened of others and new situations. In short, they were better-adjusted monkeys.

This need for "contact comfort" certainly applies to human infants as well, and is one of the many benefits that breast-feeding provides for human infants.

Close physical comforting provides emotional support for a baby, monkey or human that is essential to their emotional well-being.

9

MORAL DEVELOPMENT
AND KOHLBERG

—ɱ—

Lawrence Kohlberg developed the first major theory of human moral development. He attempted to understand how a persons "moral compass" develops as they become older, wiser, and more experienced.

Kohlberg asked people of various ages about a problem involving a moral dilemma, for example, should a person steal a drug from the pharmacist that invented it, if the drug was beyond his reach financially. The druggist selling the drug would not discount it, and was making huge profits. Without the drug, the mans wife would die.

Kohlberg discovered three levels of moral development, each consisting of two stages.

In stage 1 a child views right and wrong through the prism of "will I get punished for doing that?"

In stage 2 the person considers what might be rewarded, and what others might do.

In stage 3, a child determines what would help others, or what others approve of, and acts in a manner in accordance with those concepts.

In stage 4, a child is more apt to show obedience to authority, i.e. "it's against the law."

When a child reaches stage 5, the issue becomes more complex. The child realizes rules exist for a purpose, but that in some cases an individuals right might just supersede "the rules."

Stage 6 is the highest and most sophisticated level of human moral development. At this stage, black and white issues disappear, and many issues become various shades of grey. In this highest stage, a person follows their own ethical principles, in many cases, ones that are more stringent than those of society at large. Justice, fairness, and human dignity become factors that are weighed in moral decision-making.

According to Kohlberg, few people evolve to stage 6.

Moral development cannot be divorced from ones religious and cultural beliefs, what values an individuals parents instilled in them, or their cognitive development.

10

ERICK ERICKSON AND PSYCHOSOCIAL DEVELOPMENT

—〜〜—

Erick Erickson developed one of the most important theories of human development to date. This respected theory suggests that all people are social beings, we have different needs and priorities in each stage of our life, we have certain things we are driven to accomplish during each stage of life, and that the problems we experience in a stage may impact our adjustment in subsequent stages. All of us travel through the stages of life in the same sequence.

In each stage of life, we have something to accomplish. That challenge is our priority during that specific stage.

Below are the psychosocial stages of life put forth by Erickson. The term on the left is the positive way we hope to exit that stage. The term on the right represents the manner in which we hopefully do not exit that particular stage.

1. Trust versus Mistrust   Birth to one

During this stage of life, we learn to trust the world or we do not. It all depends on if we are nurtured, loved, and taken care of, physically and emotionally. If we are nurtured and loved during this stage, we tend to trust the world, others, and the seeds of optimism are sewn.

2. Autonomy versus Shame and Doubt   1-2

In this period of life, we learn to become autonomous. We learn to control ourselves, to delay our need for instant gratification. Toilet training occurs, a great point of pride for parent and child.

3. Initiative versus Guilt   3-5

The author witnessed a father and child at the mall one day, the little boy, of this stage of life, clearly enjoying some father-son time. The little boy saw a man without legs, and loudly asked his father, his hero and mentor, what happened to the mans legs. Father told the boy to shut up, and to not embarrass the man. This probably embarrassed the man even further, and certainly made the boy feel guilty. He certainly would think twice before taking the initiative again to ask his dad about something he found so interesting and confusing. The author does not recommend not stressing social skills and respect of others. Obviously, this situation could have been handled in such a way that the boy could have been rewarded for his initiative, and he could have been taught some social skills at the same time. Instead, the boy was made to feel guilty.

4. Competency versus Inferiority   6-12

In this stage of life, the bulk of our academic learning occurs. Education is stressed, and children know it is important. If they compare themselves favorably to others, they take with them in life a sense of competency. If not, they leave this stage with a sense of inferiority.

5. Identity versus Role Confusion   12-18

A lot is expected of young people during this stage of life. They are expected to make some big plans, set a course in life, and to do that they must be convinced that they can and will become an autonomous adult with goals and direction. A successful negotiation of this stage allows one to move on with a good sense of identity. Difficulty during this stage leads to one leaving the stage with a sense of confusion and a sense of aimlessness.

6. Intimacy versus Isolation   Young adulthood

In this stage of life, our life is orientated towards finding a person, or people, to become intimate with. A significant other, close friends, relatives, we seek their closeness and support. Problems in the trust versus mistrust stage may make this a challenge.

7. Generativity versus Stagnation   Middle age

This is when our mid-life crisis occurs. In this stage of life, we need to feel as though we have given birth to something or someone that will outlive us. We need to make a contribution that will last. It might mean nurturing our own child, mentoring a younger person in our chosen profession, or making a contribution that will last longer than we will.

8. Ego integrity versus Despair   late adulthood

In this stage, we feel a need to look back at our lives and take stock of the previous stages. If we reflect back and see all or most of our exits from each stage described by the term on the left, we reflect back with ego integrity and have a good feeling. If we assess a negative life history and see many exits from the stages of life described by the term on the right, we feel despair, and it shows.

Erickson's theory helps us understand the needs and focus of people of a different age, and helps a therapist understand issues a patient is dealing with in their specific time of life.

11

FESTINGER, COGNITIVE DISSONANCE, AND BOREDOM

—m—

People are uncomfortable if they believe two incompatible things at the same time. The discomfort they feel is called cognitive dissonance. We also feel it if our actions differ from our beliefs. We feel so uncomfortable with cognitive dissonance, that we are motivated to maintain beliefs that are consistent with one another, and we are motivated to have our deeds match our beliefs.

Festinger explored these phenomena experimentally. He had people perform a very boring task for one hour. Half of them were paid $20 for doing it, the other half were paid only $1 for doing it. The group paid only $1 when debriefed after the experiment, actually reported that they enjoyed the task. The people paid $20 to perform the task said they hated it. Why? Cognitive dissonance.

Ever wonder why recovering alcoholics are coached to talk often about their problem? Because they will have extreme cognitive dissonance if they talk a lot about not drinking, and then go out and drink.

Cognitive dissonance is a strong force that impacts human behavior

12

ELEMENTARY MY DEAR WASON.
CONFIRMATION BIAS

—m—

When we have a belief, especially a strong one, or a belief about something that is important to us, we tend to ignore information that would disprove our belief, or question the reliability of evidence that is presented to us that would refute our belief. Furthermore, we do a really good job of noticing things that support our belief, and put a great deal of weight on it, much more than we should.

Peter Wason, in the 1960's, postulated and researched these phenomena, which is now called "confirmation bias".

13

THE BYSTANDER EFFECT

—◊—

In which home will the phone be answered first, one where seven people live, or one where two people live? Common sense might suggest that it would be the home in which seven people reside. But that is not the case. *The presence of other people reduces our sense of responsibility for a situation.*

In 1964, Kitty Genovese, a resident of New York City, was brutally murdered. Thirty-eight people in the area witnessed it, and no one helped. This tragedy prompted Bibb Latane and John Darley to research the dynamics of this tragedy.

As explained above, they discovered the bystander effect.

Makes you question the effectiveness of assigning a problem to be solved to a committee.

14

ZIMBARDO AND THE PRISON

—ɯ—

In 1971 at Stanford University, Dr. Zimbardo, a professor, conducted an interesting experiment with volunteer college students. Some of the volunteers role-played prisoners, others played the role of the guards. Zimbardo himself became the warden. The experiment was conducted to study the behavior of prisoners and guards in a highly controlled experimental setting.

Zimbardo's experiment sure taught us a lot. The volunteers took their roles so seriously the experiment had to be ended prematurely. Far earlier than it was supposed to end. The guards became extraordinarily cruel, the prisoners were too combative. Had the experiment continued, someone surly would have been hurt, and Dr. Zimbardo discredited.

Zimbardo's conclusion: Often, it is the role we play that determines much of our behavior, not that which is within us.

Many years later, in 2004, Zimbardo was called as an expert witness to help defend one of the prison guards at the notorious Abu Ghraib Prison. Zimbardo explained that it is often our environment and the role we are playing that drives extreme behaviors.

15

MILGRAM AND HIS SHOCKING STUDIES

Professor Stanley Milgram wondered how the horrors of the holocaust could have happened. He set out to study people's willingness to be obedient to authority. What he found was shocking, in more ways than one.

Milgram told student volunteers that he was studying memory. One volunteer was to be the teacher, the other the student. When the student responded with a wrong answer to a question that assessed his memory, the teacher administered progressively painful shocks, despite the painful protests of the person being shocked. The shocks were portrayed as being extremely painful, even dangerous. How many volunteer teachers in the experiment administered the most powerful shock possible? 65 percent. Sixty-five percent of the teacher volunteers administered what they thought to be progressively more painful shocks to the student volunteer, despite those persons begging to quit.

As it turns out, as is often the case in social psychology experiments, there was some deception on the part of the researcher. The study was not about memory, and a person was not really being shocked. The purpose of the study was to see how many people would follow orders and be obedient to authority.

Milgram discovered that most people were willing to follow orders from an authority figure, because they thought it to be his responsibility, not theirs.

He also discovered that compliance decreased when a subject saw someone else refuse to go on.

Many of us tend to conform and follow orders if we feel we are not the ones ultimately responsible. Shocking.

This may be why soldiers are trained not to question orders.

16

STEREOTYPES

—⁂—

As a general rule, we like things to be simple. That is one of the main reasons that stereotypes exist. What is a stereotype? We develop a stereotype when we judge an entire class of people based on our experiences with one member, or just a few members, of that group, even when our experience with that one person or handful of people is quite limited. We all slip into developing stereotypes readily, though we know it is not right to do so. We maintain stereotypes over time, in spite of having experiences that should allow us to outgrow them. They are remarkably resistant to change. Sometimes we adopt stereotypes by imitation from others.

A high school student has one bad experience with a football player. She is convinced that all football players are rude and unfriendly as a result. She tells all her friends. They in turn act unfriendly towards the football players at the school. The boys on the team sense the dislike that many in the student body have for them, so they begin ignoring all of their classmates that are not on the football team. This stereotype has now become a *self-fulfilling prophecy*. Such are the dangers and dynamics of stereotypes.

Stereotypes, though unfair, are easily developed because they serve a protective function. If you believe all used car salesman are dishonest (an unfair assumption) you are less likely to be taken advantage of when you buy a used car. Stereotypes also exist because they make life easier. It is less taxing to judge an entire category of people, than it is to invest the time to get to know people individually.

A stereotype threat exists when you fear that what you do will be used by others to reinforce what stereotype they may have about you. For example, you are a female math major. Many people hold the stereotype that women are just not all that good at math. You know people hold that stereotype; it makes you somewhat anxious because you do not want to feed into it, and your performance in math class suffers as a result. This dynamic of the stereotype threat now becomes a self-fulfilling prophecy.

17

EMOTIONAL DECISION MAKING

—∿—

Is it better to make a decision with your head and not your heart? Probably not.

Dr. Antonio Damasio, a neurologist, noticed that his patients with brain damage in a specific area found it very difficult to
 make simple decisions. The area damaged was the area where the brain centers for knowledge and logic interact with emotional functioning.

Taking a multiple-choice test for a college course? If you have studied hard, prepared well, often you will do better with your gut instinct, the choice you first feel the strongest about.

Contrary to popular belief, it is often best to make decisions according to what we think and what we feel.

18

LAKE WOBEGON

Garrison Keillor the great American writer, humorist, and radio broadcaster writes often of a fictional town, Lake Wobegon where " all the women are strong, all the men are good looking, and all the children are above average." Mr. Keillor's fictional writing tells us a lot about how we tend to perceive ourselves.

Generally, we view ourselves as being better than other people. If we are an attorney, we feel our legal acumen is better than that of our legal colleagues. If play baseball for a living, we tend to feel that our ability to play the game is better than that of our professional peers. We feel we are better looking than the person sitting next to us. In short, we generally feel we are superior to others. We are "legends in our own minds."

These phenomena used to be called illusory superiority. We now call it the Lake Wobegon effect.

There is a flip side to this though. It is called the worse than average effect. This means we tend to underestimate our abilities to do novel or unusual tasks, and that we compare ourselves very unfavorably to others in these novel areas.

We tend to think we are smarter than all our neighbors, but the worst unicycle rider in the world.

19

FUNDAMENTAL ATTRIBUTION ERROR

—ᚲ—

Whenever we see someone do something, or hear someone say something, we always attempt to attach an explanation to his or her behavior. Why did they do that? Because they are a good (or bad) person, or because the situation forced them into acting in a particular way?

If we determine that a person behaved the way they did because that is just the kind of person they are on the inside, we have made an internal attribution. If we feel they acted the way they did because the situation forced them to, we are making an external attribution.

You have a favorite newspaper columnist. You like his column because he is a liberal, just like you. You have read him for twenty years. One day, he writes a very conservative column, which you dislike. You are disappointed and stop reading him because you feel he is really a conservative on the inside. You have just made an internal attribution. You never stopped to think that he works for a very conservative paper, and perhaps he was ordered to write an article espousing that particular line of thought. Had you considered that explanation, you would have made an external attribution.

Generally, we tend to make internal attributions far more than we should. In other words, we tend to assume people do things because that is who they are on the inside. We usually fail to consider that the situation they are in forced them to behave in a certain way. When we make this mistake that is what is called the fundamental attribution error, something all of us do much more often than we should. People do this to us as well. Keep that in mind.

One additional note, we also tend to assume that people act in the way they do for the same reasons we would. This too is often inaccurate. They may engage in the same actions we do, but often their motives can be different than ours.

20

PAVLOV AND HIS SALIVATING DOGS

—〰—

Ivan Pavlov was a Russian physiologist that stumbled upon an important finding in the field of psychology. Though Pavlov swore up and down he was not a psychologist, nonetheless, he is generally recognized as one of the top ten people in the field of psychology in terms of his influence.

Pavlov studied the digestive system of dogs. He discovered that when a dog sees food, the dog salivates. It does not have to be taught to do so, it just does.

Whenever food was presented to dogs in his study, a bell would ring. The presentation of food and the ringing of the bell were paired together so much, that soon the dog learned to salivate just to the sound of the bell even when food was not presented.

What happened here is what we now call classical conditioning, a very simple form of learning.

Pavlov's concept of classical conditioning allows us to understand basic learning that occurs even in humans.

Every time you sit in a dentist's chair you are poked, prodded, and generally tortured. The day may come when you need to come in just to talk with your dentist. You know before hand that she will not be coming anywhere near your mouth, you will just be talking. Dental offices are not well appointed with furniture, so you have to sit in that same treatment chair when you talk with the dentist. You sit in that chair and you begin to feel anxious. Why? That chair has been paired with pain so much that you have been conditioned to feel anxious in it.

Classical conditioning, a form of learning, explains many behaviors, including many phobias that people may have.

Remember to brush and floss.

21

MASLOW HIS TRIANGLE AND OUR HIERARCHY OF NEEDS

—m—

Abraham Maslow was a humanistic psychologist. He believed that people are basically good, and that they want to become the best people they can be, and, along the way, be good to others.

Maslow felt that we all have needs. Picture our needs as being represented graphically on a triangle. At the base of the triangle we have basic needs of warmth, food, and basic necessities. When those needs are met, we desire to meet the next set of needs on this triangle, safety. Then come belonging-ness, then esteem, self-esteem, and finally self-actualization, which means becoming the best person we can become in all aspects of our life. The best father, son, uncle, brother, accountant, neighbor, stamp collector, and gardener we can become.

According to Maslow, we all are just trying to become the best person we can be; we all want to become self-actualized. This explains our behavior and our motivation.

22

GROUPTHINK AND JANIS

—m—

Dr. Irving Janis of Yale University has postulated the existence of a very important human dynamic now known as groupthink.

When you get a group of people together, even if they are extraordinarily intelligent, often they will make some rather stupid, or even extreme decisions. How can this happen? Groupthink.

When people are charged with the responsibility of making a decision as a group, are insulated from people from outside of the group, and know the position or desire of their leader, often they will make some very extreme decisions that no individual in the group would have made on their own. As they explore the problem, there is an emphasis on loyalty, consensus, being a team player, and pleasing the leader. The group has little concern about the practicality or workability of their recommendations, and often will not tolerate anyone attempting to play the devils advocate.

The dynamic of groupthink often leads to poor and extreme positions recommended by the group. The Bay of Pigs fiasco has been blamed on the groupthink phenomena.

The cure: the leader should not tell an advisory group his or her opinions, dissent should be encouraged, and the group should not be so insular. All members should feel free to act as a devils advocate, and no one should be criticized for questioning the appropriateness of any of the recommendations the group is considering.

23

THE PLACEBO EFFECT

—w—

Often, if we are ill, with either physical or mental illness, we will get better if we think we will get better. Our condition often improves, in part, if we expect it to.

When a new drug is being developed, it goes through test trials. The pool of subjects the new drug is being tested with is divided into two groups. One group gets the real medication that is being researched, and the other group gets a worthless pill, often a sugar pill, that is called a placebo.

The improvement in these two groups is compared. The people in these groups do not know if they received the real medication or the phony medication (the placebo). Further, the doctors evaluating the improvement in the patients do not know which drug the patient received. Both the doctors and the patients are "blind" as to which medication (real or phony) is being dispensed. Such as study is called a "double blind study", the gold standard of good scientific research.

Why is research conducted in this manner? Because often people improve if they think they are going to improve. That is called the placebo effect. If the people that received the real medication improve significantly more than the people that received the sugar pill (placebo), the placebo effect does not appear to be the reason the patient improved. It is probable their condition improved because they were taking the real medication.

Outside of such research studies the placebo effect is still important. People taking morphine without knowing they are being given a pain killer will have some improvement in that they will suffer less pain. That same patient will experience more pain relief, however, if he knows that he is receiving a painkiller. This too is the placebo effect.

The placebo effect is relevant not only with medication, but is a powerful force even in talk therapy.

We often will get better, or feel better, at least to some degree, if we feel we should be getting better.

24

THE FLYNN EFFECT

—ww—

We are getting smarter. IQ scores are increasing in modern times at a pretty brisk clip. Compared to folks a century ago, we are downright brilliant. A professor from New Zealand named Flynn discovered this trend; hence it is dubbed "The Flynn Effect."

Remember, we are talking about IQ scores here. There is some debate about if IQ scores and intelligence are one in the same, but that is an argument for a different book.

What are some of the reasons for the Flynn Effect? Technology? Students are exposed to a great deal of technology now, and literally have the world at their fingertips. In fact, they often have to teach their parents how to use this technology. Educational techniques have improved. Critical and abstract thinking are being emphasized much more than ever before. Perhaps it is just the evolution of our species. It may be due to more gender equality.

Whatever the reasons, it is a good phenomena. The Flynn Effect is certainly being researched and evaluated. Some research suggests that this trend may have stopped.

Stay tuned.

25

'THE BIG FIVE"

—⚝—

Personality is "the complex of characteristics that distinguishes an individual." In other words, our personality consists of the traits we have that others take note of. These traits make us distinctly us.

Psychology has many theories of personality, but one stands out from the others. It is referred to as the "Big Five" theory of personality. This theory suggests that an individual's personality can best be described by understanding where they are at on the continuum of five major traits. Think of these traits as a continuum. One can posses a great deal of each characteristic, or very little of each characteristic. In most cases, a person would fall somewhere in the middle in each of these trait continuums. The five traits that best describe ones personality according to the "Big Five" theory are as follows:

1. Extraversion (how outgoing we are.)
2. Neuroticism (how anxious, fearful, or apprehensive we are.)
3. Conscientiousness (can we delay our need for immediate gratification and work hard, do what needs to be done.)
4. Openness (are we open to new ideas, are we creative?)
5. Agreeableness (do we "play well" with others, get along with others, "go with the flow"?)

According to the Big Five perspective, you can understand just who a person is if you are aware of where they are at on each of these continuums of traits.

26

NATURE VERSUS NURTURE

—ᵥᵥ—

Do our genes determine who will we become, or does our environment? Both actually. Certainly genes are important. If you have a blood relative with a psychological disorder, you may be *genetically predisposed* to that disorder, be more at risk to suffer from it than someone that does not have it in their family history, *if* a stressor in the environment "turns on" that genetic predisposition. It does not mean that you will definitely have to deal with having this problem, just that you are more likely to be challenged with it if your environment stresses you in certain ways.

Science now suggests to us that a person is born with their sexual orientation. That the environment does not "turn them gay." If you have a gay sibling, you are more likely to have that sexual orientation than if you do not have a gay sibling. Having a gay sibling does not mean you too will be gay, it does mean that, statistically, you are more likely to have that sexual orientation than someone that does not have a gay sibling.

Autism, once thought not to have a genetic component, does seem to have one. If you have an autistic blood relative, you are more likely to be on the autism spectrum yourself.

Intelligence certainly has a genetic component, but here is no question that environment plays a significant role in ones intelligence level.

In most cases, most attributes we have are impacted by both heredity and environment. A doctor, a lawyer, a beggar man or thief is both born and made, to some degree. Heredity and environment interact to determine who we are.

Recently, the study of *epigenetics* suggests that in some cases our experiences may actually alter our genes. Now that is a real interaction between heredity and environment.

27

HYSTERICAL CHARCOT

—ɯ—

Jean-Martin Charcot in some ways was an inspiration to Sigmund Freud. Charcot discovered that some people that seemed to have some very serious neurological problems such as seizures or paralysis had nothing wrong with them neurologically. Though their problems were "all in their head", they were very real nonetheless. Patients at the time with physical problems that had no physical cause were called "hysterical".

Charcot suggested that unconscious forces were responsible for such maladies.

Freud later stated that such hysterical illness was due to unconscious repressed memories, perhaps of a traumatic event. Pierre Janet suggested that hysterical illnesses might be due to the mind compartmentalizing different functions.

It was Charcot that originally discovered that unconscious forces within us could cause actual physical problems.

28

WE FOLLOW OUR LEADER

—◊◊◊—

Do we follow our leaders? Generally, yes. Are we more likely to follow a leader that is the most capable, the smartest, or the best at what they do? Not necessarily. Social identity theory suggests that we often follow people we perceive to be just like us. Ever wonder why politicians go out of their way to portray themselves as being just an ordinary guy? Because they understand this.

A leader that looks like us, acts like us, or dresses like us is more likely to find followers. In times of crisis, we draw closer to people we share similarities with, and trust them more to lead us. When the chips are down, it always seems like it is "us" versus "them." We need to clearly perceive our leader as being one of "us."

29

FALSE MEMORIES

—⚇—

Karen Loftus conducted some interesting research on memory. She interviewed her research subject's parents to get information about the person, recounted the information to the person in her study, but added a story that was not true, that the person was lost in a shopping mall when he or she was a little kid. About twenty-five percent of the subjects not only indicated that they remember having been lost in the mall, but also incorporated this made up incident into stories they told about their childhood. Were they lying? No. They simply incorporated this incident into their memories because they trusted the source of the story.

Our memories are highly malleable and subject to change. Over the years we may add to them.

In another study, people were asked to read a short ghost story twice. Then they were asked to recount the story in their own words. Many people talked about things that were not in the story, they tended to be events that they expected to be in a typical ghost story.

We are highly suggestible, as are our memories. Sometimes, a "memory" that is recounted has more to do with how the question was asked, then what actually happened.

If a young child is asked repeatedly about possible abuse that did not occur, sometimes they may "remember" that abuse.

Memory is not always accurate. Often, when we are older, when we share a memory, we may incorporate other people's stories into our account of the event.

30

BEHAVIORISM FEATURING WATSON AND SKINNER

Behaviorism is a major school of thought in the field of psychology today, and has been for some time. Two of its most prominent adherents were John B. Watson and B.F.

Skinner. Behaviorism has two main tenants:

1. Psychology is a science, and should be empirical.
2. Behavior is a result of its consequences.

Behaviorists feel that psychology should concern itself with the observable, testable, and verifiable. Therefore, less observable things such as mental processes or ones emotional feelings are often not the subject of research emphasis.

Behaviorists also are of the opinion that behavior is a result of its consequences. We behave the way we do because there has been a payoff of sorts for our having behaved in that particular fashion. Conversely, we do not engage in certain behaviors that have resulted in negative consequences.

Those that adhere to the behavioral school of thought recognize the importance of operant conditioning in terms of explaining behavior and learning. Want your child to learn to share with others? Praise them when you catch them sharing. This praise will act as a positive reinforcer (reward) for their sharing behavior, and make it more likely that they will share in the future.

Do you want to house train your dog? Give it a treat when he relieves himself outside. Or, punish him when he experiences an accident inside. A positive reinforcement by its onset increases the frequency of the behavior that it immediately follows. A punishment by its onset decreases the frequency of the behavior that it immediately follows.

Behaviors that have been taught by operant conditioning (the use of applying consequences such as positive reinforcement or punishment) must be maintained by occasional reinforcement or the behaviors may drop out of the organism's behavioral repertoire. When that happens, the behavior is said to be extinguished.

Learning, according to behaviorists, occurs because of our reinforcement history. For example, as a child's babbling more closely resembles human speech, the baby is rewarded by smiles, hugs and attention, and this reinforcement helps speech develop.

The behaviors we exhibit, and even the beliefs we have, exist because they have been rewarded over time according to the behaviorists. Behavior is a result of its consequences.

THE HISTORY OF PSYCHOLOGY: A TIMELINE

430 BCE   Hippocrates states that mental illness is due to an imbalance of the four major body fluids.

350 BCE   Aristotle writes about the relationship between the soul and the body

1649   Descartes writes *The Passion of the Soul* in which he postulates that the pineal gland is where our soul resides.

1848   Phineas Gage, an unlucky laborer receives brain damage from an accident. Scientists of the time study the effect of this brain damage on his behavior.

1858   Charles Darwin publishes an article about natural selection.

1879   Wilhelm Wundt founds the first psychological research laboratory.

1884   The James-Lange theory of emotion is proposed.

1890   William James publishes the first psychology textbook, *Principles of Psychology*.

1900   Sigmund Freud publishes *The Interpretation of Dreams*.

1904	Spearman writes about a general factor of intelligence.
1905	Freud announces his theory of psychosexual personality development.
1905	Binet and Simon develop the first IQ test to predict success in school.
1906	Ivan Pavlov announces his findings and explains classical conditioning.
1906	Ramon y Cajal discovers that the nervous system is composed of individual cells.
1911	Thorndike announces the law of effect
1913	Carl Jung announces his theory of the collective unconscious
1915	Freud postulates the idea of defense mechanisms.
1920	Watson conducts the "Little Albert" experiment
1921	Allport puts forth a trait theory of personality.
1921	The first neurotransmitter is discovered.
1921	Herman Rorshach develops a landmark projective technique, the inkblot test.

1930   Jean Piaget, a cognitive theorist, announces a theory of cognitive development and delineates four stages of cognitive development.

1934   Lev Vygotsky explains his Zone of Proximal Development

1935   Henry Murray develops the Thematic Apperception Test, another projective technique

1938   Electroconvulsive shock is first used with a human patient.

1938   BF Skinner lays out the principles of operant conditioning.

1942   Carl Rogers explains client-centered therapy.

1942   The Minnesota Multiphasic Personality Inventory is published.

1950   Erick Erickson contributes his theory on the stages of psychosocial development.

1951   Asch does his study on conformity.

1952   The first edition of the *Diagnostic and Statistical Manual for Diagnosing Mental Disorders* is published.

1954   Abraham Maslow puts forth his hierarchy of needs to explain human motivation.

1956   Hans Seyle explains the General Adaptation Syndrome, a framework explaining the human response to stress.

1959   Harlowe publishes his study detailing the importance of contact comfort in monkeys.

1963   Albert Bandura conducts his "Bobo Doll" study.

1963   Stanley Milgram completes his study on obedience to authority.

1963   Kohlberg puts forth his theory of moral development.

1967   Learned helplessness is explained by Seligman.

1968   Hemispheric specialization in split-brain patients is studied by Sperry.

1974   Type A Personalities are found to have more heart disease.

1977   Thomas and Chess explain the different types of temperaments that children have.

1978   Elizabeth Loftus publishes research on the misinformation effect.

1979   The Minnesota twin studies using twins that are raised apart begins in an effort to study the effects of heredity and environment on a variety of human characteristics.

1981   David Wechsler begins to develop IQ tests for highly specific age groups.

1983	Gardner announces his theory of multiple intelligences.
1985	Sternberg publishes his theory of triarchic intelligence.
1995	Golman puts forth a theory of emotional intelligence.
1997	Elizabeth Kubler-Ross expands her theory on death and dying and proposes the five stages of death.
2000	The Human Genome Project is completed.
2005	Storch proposes the use of stem cells to repair damaged neural tissue.
2008	By law, health insurance companies in the United States must cover mental illness at the same levels as physical illness.
2009	Barack Obama removes limits on federal funding for stem cell research.
2014	DSM-V will be published.

CPSIA information can be obtained at www.ICGtesting.com
Printed in the USA
LVOW10s2207110813

347359LV00002B/116/P

9 781481 028189